THIRD EYE

By Harvey Stuart

Copyright © 2017 by Harvey Stuart

All Rights Reserved. This document is geared towards providing exact and reliable information in regards to the topic and issue covered. The publication is sold with the idea that the publisher is not required to render accounting, officially permitted, or otherwise, qualified services. If advice is necessary, legal or professional, a practiced individual in the profession should be ordered.

- From a Declaration of Principles which was accepted and approved equally by a Committee of the American Bar Association and a Committee of Publishers and Associations.

In no way is it legal to reproduce, duplicate, or transmit any part of this document in either electronic means or in printed format. Recording of this publication is strictly prohibited and any storage of this document is not allowed unless with written permission from the publisher. All rights reserved.

The information provided herein is stated to be truthful and consistent, in that any liability, in terms of inattention or otherwise, by any usage or abuse of any policies, processes, or directions contained within is the solitary and utter responsibility of the recipient reader. Under no circumstances will any legal responsibility or blame be held against the publisher for any reparation, damages, or monetary loss due to the information herein, either directly or indirectly.

Respective authors own all copyrights not held by the publisher.

The information herein is offered for informational purposes solely, and is universal as so. The presentation of the information is without contract or any type of guarantee assurance.

The trademarks that are used are without any consent, and the publication of the trademark is without permission or backing by the trademark owner. All trademarks and brands within this book are for clarifying purposes only and are the owned by the owners themselves, not affiliated with this document.

Disclaimer and Terms of Use: The Author and Publisher has strived to be as accurate and complete as possible in the creation of this book, notwithstanding the fact that he does not warrant or represent at any time that the contents within are accurate due to the rapidly changing nature of the Internet. While all attempts have been made to verify information provided in this publication, the Author and Publisher assumes no responsibility for errors, omissions, or contrary interpretation of the subject matter herein.

Any perceived slights of specific persons, peoples, or organizations are unintentional. In practical advice books, like anything else in life, there are no guarantees of results. Readers are cautioned to rely on their own judgment about their individual circumstances and act accordingly.

This book is not intended for use as a source of legal, medical, business, accounting or financial advice. All readers are advised to seek services of competent professionals in the legal, medical, business, accounting, and finance fields.

BEST MEATLOAF RECIPES

TABLE OF CONTENTS

Introduction 5

Third Eye Meditation 11

How To Open Your Third Eye 16

Experiences After The Third Eye Opening 21

What to expect after the third eye opening 22

Third Eye – FAQ 31

Third Eye Chakra Healing 34

Benefits of Opening Your Third Eye 45

INTRODUCTION

The third eye is one of the seven chakras in our chakra system. Anyone can learn how to "open" their third eye using their innate psychic ability. The third eye chakra, sometimes also referred to as the mind center, is our road to wisdom, spirituality and inner vision. For this reason many psychics see it as being the most important chakra. Learning to open the third eye will allow you to access spiritual guidance. It can be a long process learning how to open the third eye. You will only really know that you have been successful when you have actually achieved it. Don't give up if you do not have quick success, because it will be very beneficial and enlightening when you achieve it.

One way of harnessing your psychic ability to open your third eye is through meditation and chanting. You can gradually introduce the chanting into meditation that you usually do. The chakras have different "seed sounds". You can learn the seed sound for the third eye chakra and chant it softly. This will have the effect of stimulating the third eye chakra and with patience may help you to open it. It is a very good idea to use the chant alongside your usual meditation practice and focus on the third eye chakra while you are chanting and meditating. This will create the right conditions for the third eye to be able to open.

In order to get into the right state of mind you need to find a comfortable position. Try the same time and place as you would usually meditate. This will be best for you as you will be naturally comfortable and relaxed and your psychic ability will be able to be used to its full benefit. You probably close your eyes whilst meditating and this is generally a good idea when focusing on the third eye chakra as it takes away any distracting visual stimuli. The chant for the third eye chakra sounds like a long "ooooh" sound ending in a shorter "mmm" hum sound. While you are chanting you will need to keep focused on the third eye. The third eye chakra is located at the center of your forehead. It is important to focus on your third eye for the meditation to succeed.

With patience and practice and the application of your psychic ability you will find that this method allows you to open your third eye. Do not give up. Even though success may take some time to come the process on its own is hugely beneficial for your spiritual well being. When you are successful you will not need to be told, you will feel that your third eye has opened.

WHAT IS THE THIRD EYE CHAKRA?

The third eye chakra is the sixth chakra. Located on the forehead, between the eyebrows, it is the center of intuition and foresight. The function of the third eye chakra is driven by the principle of openness and imagination.

THIRD EYE CHAKRA MEANING

The fifth chakra is referred to as:

* Third eye chakra

* Brow chakra

* Ajna chakra

* Bhru Madhya

* Dvidak Padma

The most common Sanskrit name for the Third eye chakra is "Ajna", which means "command" and "perceiving".

This chakra is related to the "supreme element", which is the combination of all the elements in their pure form.

Yogic meaning of the 3rd eye chakra

In yogic metaphysics, the third eye or Ajna chakra, is the center where we transcend duality – the duality of a personal "I" separate from the rest of the world, of a personality that exists independently from everything else.

One more thing… Restoring the power of your chakras is about how you can take back control of your health and wellness by learning to work with energy.

This is life-changing material.

You can use Energy Medicine to…

* Lessen aches, pains, illness, and disease

* Create deeper happiness, satisfaction, and contentment

* Increase focus, clarity, and productivity

* Renew balance, health, harmony, and well-being

You'll see what we mean when you join this new Masterclass with energy healer Donna Eden. You can use what you'll learn in this class to… heal yourself, create happiness, look good, and improve longevity. And all it takes is a few simple non-invasive hand gestures!

THIRD EYE CHAKRA COLOR

The third eye chakra is most commonly represented with the color purple or bluish purple. The auric color of third eye chakra energy can also be seen as translucent purple or bluish white.

Rather than by its color, it is characterized by the quality of its luminescence or soft radiance that reminds us of the moon light.

THIRD EYE CHAKRA SYMBOL

The image of the Third Eye chakra symbol contains two elements frequently associated with wisdom: the upside down triangle and the lotus flower.

THIRD EYE CHAKRA LOCATION

The most commonly accepted location for the sixth chakra is between the eyebrows, slightly above at the bridge of your nose.

Contrary to a common misconception, it is not located in the middle of the forehead, but between the eyes where the eyebrows would meet. It can also be described as being located behind the eyes in the middle of the head. Note that secondary chakras run along the midline of the forehead, but the third eye chakra is typically located lower.

The Third eye chakra is associated to the pineal gland in charge of regulating biorhythms, including sleep and wake time. It's a gland located in the brain that is a center of attention because of its relationship with the perception and effect of light and altered or "mystical" states of consciousness. It's positioned close to the optical nerves, and as such, sensitive to visual stimulations and changes in lighting.

BEHAVIORAL CHARACTERISTICS OF THE THIRD EYE CHAKRA

The third eye chakra is associated with the following psychological and behavioral characteristics:

* Vision

* Intuition

* Perception of subtle dimensions and movements of energy

* Psychic abilities related to clairvoyance and clairaudience especially

* Access to mystical states, illumination

* Connection to wisdom, insight

* Motivates inspiration and creativity

The third eye chakra is an instrument to perceive the more subtle qualities of reality. It goes beyond the more physical senses into the realm of subtle energies. Awakening your third eye allows you to open up to an intuitive sensibility and inner perception.

Because it connects us with a different way of seeing and perceiving, the third eye chakra's images are often hard to describe verbally. It puts us in touch with the ineffable and the intangible more closely. Third eye visions are also often more subtle than regular visions: They may appear a bit "blurry", ghost-like, cloudy, or dream-like. Sometimes however, the inner visions might be clear like a movie playing in front of your eyes.

Sustaining awareness of third eye chakra energy might require focus and the ability to relax into a different way of seeing.

When we focus our mind and consciousness, we can see beyond the distractions and illusions that stand before us and have more insight to live and create more deeply aligned with our highest good. The third eye chakra is associated with the archetypal dimensions, as well as the realm of spirits.

THIRD EYE CHAKRA IMBALANCE

When the Third eye chakra has an imbalance, it can manifest as:

* Feeling stuck in the daily grind without being able to look beyond your problems and set a guiding vision for yourself

* Overactive third chakra without support from the rest of the chakra system may manifest as fantasies that appear more real than reality, indulgence in psychic fantasies and illusions

* Not being able to establish a vision for oneself and realize it

* Rejection of everything spiritual or beyond the usual

* Not being able to see the greater picture

* Lack of clarity

THIRD EYE MEDITATION

Third eye meditation is one of the many enigmatic concepts that have befuddled the human mind from centuries. This type of meditation primarily focuses on the ajna (brow) chakra according to Hindu spirituality.

According to Hindu mythology, Lord Shiva, the destroyer of the universe possesses the 'Third Eye' which is located between his eyebrows and a little higher than the bridge of the nose. Whenever the universe is threatened by the immoral atrocities committed by mankind, the sacred energy of the third eye engages and burns down the evil to ashes. When Lord Shiva calms down aftermath, he lets the generative energy flow through his third eye to create a new universe.

Through third eye meditation, you establish contact with your inner energies and accumulate them to help you advance to higher levels of spiritual consciousness. You acquire the wisdom to distinguish the layers of this material world and beyond.

To practice third eye meditation, find a quiet and comfortable place. Sit down and take a few deep breaths. Open the doors and windows of your mind and let all the troubling thoughts and feelings escape.

Close your eyes. While breathing in and out, concentrate on the region between your eyebrows i.e. the third eye. Visualize your deep breathing activate this space. Believe that your third eye is a gateway to the state of realization: where you can allow the conscious to expand beyond the earthly levels.

Feel the freedom that comes with the higher knowledge. Let your spirit lose to taste the waters of the deepest seas and scale the height of the highest peaks! As you delve to search the meaning of your existence, you experience a connection with you mind through your third eye. Remain in contact with your mind and still allow your soul to travel to the places that you cannot possibly imagine exist in the material world.

Now, you are in a state where nothing: no thought, emotion or situation, can snatch away this moment: the celebration of stillness, contentment and happiness. Take some deep breaths and let your mind absorb the calmness and allow it to enter the complex layers of the unconscious. Listen to the voices within, the ones you may have left unheard in the hullabaloo of your busy life. Let these voices resonate with every particle of your mind.

With some more deep breaths, let your body and soul slowly be engulfed by the liberated energy. This energy travels from your third eye down to the other parts of the body, sending positive sensations to your spine, moving down to your feet and the soles of your feet. Now, imagine this energy flow link you back to the daily chores of your 'regular' life. But now, you're calmer and stronger to face the challenges for you possess the divine knowledge grasped through the third eye.

This sense of being alive from within empowers you to transmit this energy to other people around you. Allow others to also discover the answers to their innumerable questions by spreading the message of third eye meditation.

The practice of third eye meditation is very easy to understand. On your forehead, above your nose and in between your eyebrows, is a spot which is often called the "third eye." In third eye meditation, you concentrate on that spot with concentrated visualization. The purpose is to bring chi or prana to a dormant chakra, or energy center, which is located right at that spot. When it opens we say that you have tentatively succeeded at third eye meditation.

The visualization that you perform on this spot is usually a picture of a little diamond, silver flame, white moon, a Sanskrit letter, a Hebrew letter, a Buddha, or some other auspicious silverish or bright white figure. The principle is that when you concentrate on a region inside or outside of your body, the chi energies of your body will tend to go to that point. Because the chi or natal energy of your body goes to a particular point, it will mass in that region and when it masses, it will open up the chi channels and chakras in that area because of the friction.

Let's take another example that you can easily understand. You can visualize any of the bones in your body by imagining the shape of the bone and that its color is bright white. In time, with continued practice you will send the chi or energy of your body to the bone. This will often cause the bone to seem to glow inside your mind. By sending energy to a bone in this way, you can also banish sickness and pain. If you suffer from arthritis, this often improves the pain in a bad area. All you have to do in your visualization practice is concentrate on a region inside the body and thereby send the body physical energy to a mass at that point.

When it comes to the region of the third eye you are performing the very same function. But why should you do this at the region of the third eye? That's because the third eye is the location of a chakra in the body called the two-petalled "Ajna" charka. This is a major upper termination point of the chi channels (acupuncture meridians) in the body that stretch all the way from the perineum up your back and to the front of your head. When you concentrate on that point because of the visualization, you will tend to send the chi to that area which will in turn help to open up the chakra in that region.

It is very easy for people to develop slight psychic abilities from doing the technique. In Anthroposophy, for instance, people often visualize the stages of germination of seeds at this point in order to help open up the chakra. In Tibetan Buddhism, many people are advised to visualize a bright image at this point, within their throat, behind the breastbone and in their bellies. Many spiritual schools have similar visualization teachings to open up chakras.

However some people who do this visualization never experience any psychic effects whatsoever. The reason is because in order to power the Ajna chakra of the third eye, the chi energy (known as prana in Indian yoga) from the lower regions of the body has to ascend upward. If all the chi channels stretching from below to above are blocked or obstructed, which is normally the case, then very little energy will ever reach the third eye no matter how much visualization practice you do. You have to practice a long time to first open up these other channels as well. That's why only advanced meditators who have practiced meditation for years, and whose chi channels or acupuncture meridians are thereby somewhat cleansed because of the prior practices, experience any of the psychic abilities that are often reported to occur from this practice.

The reason that you practice this method, however, is not to develop psychic abilities. The main reason you want to practice it so that your chi from down below will enter the region of the head and help quiet your mind so that you can enter an advanced meditative state called samadhi. That's why this technique is often practiced in Taoism and in yoga. But it's also practice in Esoteric Buddhism, western alchemy, and Sufism. The purpose is not so that you develop psychic abilities so that you can see spirits and ghosts and other beings made of Chi, but so that you can learn one-pointed concentration and let go of your view of being a body. Concentrating on the Third eye through meditation is just another way of trying to bring about this spiritual result and enter the real spiritual path.

And Real Insight is available, but before you can achieve it, you have to recognize and accept the fallibility of your perception.

Perception implies a way of looking at something... just one person's point of view. There is nothing wrong with you or others having a given perspective on anything (in fact it is very challenging not to)... but if you cling to your own too tightly, or resist contrary opinions too strongly, it will prevent you from going beyond perception... and only by transcending perspective and opinion can real Truth be revealed.

Truth reveals itself once all blocks to its realization have been removed.

This is the True opening of the third eye. Real discernment of people, events, attitudes, and emotions. This is the Real ability to see through lies with little concern for the fact that someone wasn't being honest.

HOW TO OPEN YOUR THIRD EYE

Want to unlock your psychic abilities and inner vision? Learning how to open the third eye chakra is the gateway to unlocking these special powers that we all naturally possess. In this article, I am going to show you one of the techniques that helped me accomplish this but first I would like to explain in more detail exactly what the third eye chakra is and what it does. It has been discovered that each and every one of us possess seven chakras located throughout the body. The third eye, is the sixth of these seven, and is located at the center of the forehead. It is the center of all psychic powers and higher intuition. With an opened third eye chakra, you can effectively tune into your higher self.

Not everybody knows that we actually have three eyes. We humans have two physical eyes but we also have a spiritual third eye also known as Anja chakra and this eye is just as important as the two physical ones we have. There have been reports of those who have accessed their third eye they have had visions or even an astral projection. People that are able to access their third eye are also called "seers". Now to actually access your third eye it's a hard process but well worth it.

There are many different techniques when it comes to opening your third eye. A couple of the most common ways is in meditation. First things first you are going to want to sit in a comfortable potion and pretty much try to daydream. So you want to focus on that the peaceful place in your mind. It will take some time to find that place it may not come with the first try but it will happen if you stay focused and relaxed. Once you have found that your mind is clear and in the place of peace you will find where the third eye is, make sure to breathe in and out to keep yourself at the relaxed state. You will start to feel the relaxing sensation and a bit energized this is when you have awakened your chakra.

So now with this relaxation and energy your third eye should be visible to you. They say that once you have got in touch with your Anja chakra it is your body and mind working together as one making a big powerful harmonious sensory organ. Now that you have accessed your third eye it is a multi- sensory organ so it will perceive energy patterns or frequencies. It will also relay the data back in overlays information on top of your other senses. Once your third eye is open it is a very powerful ability and can give you a grander understanding of yourself and the relationship you have with the universe. However, those individuals with lower vibrations and low auras may benefit from study. It has been said that if you don't understand and develop correctly it can confuse and make you very lost in your mind.

People who have lack of understanding they tend to run away or try and hide from the ability or strange descriptions. To have it opened it opens up your awareness for many different phenomenon around us. Psychics and seers use this ability to make connections and answer questions. There has been many ways the third eye has been used to improve your life, give insight into your path and obtain universal wisdom.

The concept of opening the Third Eye is really about stimulating the pineal gland in the base of the brain. It is believed by some to be a dormant organ that can be awakened to enable "telepathic" communication and an awareness of things not perceived by the natural senses.

In the physical body the eye views objects upside down. It sends the image of what it observes to the brain which interprets the image and makes it appear right side-up to us. But the human body has another physical eye which 'sees' things, whose function has long been recognized by humanity. It is called the 'Third Eye' and like an eye, needs to be "opened". It is long thought to have mystical powers. Many consider it the Spiritual Third Eye, our Inner Vision.

When the pineal gland awakens one feels a pressure at the base of the brain. This pressure will often be experienced when connecting to higher frequency. A head injury can also activate the Third Eye (Pineal Gland). Development of psychic talents has been closely associated with this organ of higher vision.

To activate the 'third eye' and perceive higher dimensions, the pineal and pituitary glands must vibrate in unison, which is achieved through specific meditation and relaxation techniques. When the right relationship is established between personality, operating through the body, and the soul, operating through the pineal gland, a magnetic field is created. The negative and positive forces interact and become strong enough to create a phenomenon known as the 'light in the head.'

THREE STEPS TO OPENING THE THIRD EYE!

1. **- Deep Relaxation:** To even gain a basic level or clarity, you have learn how to deeply relax. Most people think they are already relaxed. They are wrong. This isn't a skill that most people are taught. It isn't difficult to learn, but before you can begin to learn it you have to recognize that you have something to learn. Deep breathing combined with simple awareness is an excellent method of learning relaxation. Practice noticing tension in your body and letting it go. Once you are comfortable doing this in a relaxing environment, begin practicing it while standing... and then while walking.

2. **- Radical Self Honesty:** Most people have ingrained the habit of lying to themselves so deeply, that there is little hope of ever letting it go. If you are still reading after that last sentence, I do have some good news for you: you are probably one of the few who is capable of learning self honesty. Here is where to start. When you are by yourself with little chance of being disturbed, state out loud: "I have chosen everything in my life. I continue to choose everything in my life. Moving forward, I will do so consciously." As you move forward in your life, do your best to live this intent.

3. **- Radical Forgiveness:** In spite of our tendency for deception, we are all really doing the best we know how to do. This includes you. To gain insight, you have to surrender old habits... but there is no reason to condemn yourself or others for having them. As you let go of your addiction to being right, forgive yourself for having it, and forgive others for having it as well... even those that seem to really enjoy shoving their assumption of correctness in your face. Let go. Forgive.

These three steps are actually all meditations in and of themselves. You can spend many years investigating the self (and life) with any one of these... and you can get a lot out of just committing to start. Set your intent to live the three third eye meditations listed above, and you will begin to open yourself to insights.

STICK WITH THIS FOR A LITTLE WHILE, AND YOU WILL NOTICE 2 THINGS:

You have become very happy and healthy.

You will start recognizing something beyond opinion arising from time to time... this is sometimes referred to as Insight (when this happens, do your best to enjoy it without clinging to it). This doesn't mean you are done, it just means you are doing good. Keep going.

Here is one insight that may help you on your path: Real Truth is radically subjective. It can't be spoken... it can only be experienced (although it can be spoken about).

Taoists have a saying that Bruce Lee summarized in the movie, Enter The Dragon:

"It is like a finger pointing to the moon... don't focus on the finger or you will miss all the heavenly glory!"

As you begin to allow your third eye to open, you too can become that finger pointing to the moon. Perceptions, opinions, beliefs, and ideas (and even the words in this article) can all potentially point at Real Truth... but you have to be willing to look beyond them in order to gain real Insight.

EXPERIENCES AFTER THE THIRD EYE OPENING

After the third eye opening you may get some unusual experiences.

Some of the experiences you may get are pleasant, some aren't. If you already opened the third eye, read about the experiences after the third eye opening. If your your third eye is not opened, read this section of the eBook.

How to know that you awakened your third eye

You can be assured that your third eye is awakened if you close your eyes and can see:

* White/blue/purple colours

* Intense white dots

* Black sky with numerous stars

* The shape of the eye/square/circle/some other shape filled with blue or purple colour

These are all signs that you've awakened your third eye.

If you feel the pressure or some activity in your third eye chakra, that means that your third eye is being awakened and soon you'll be able to see with it.

WHAT TO EXPECT AFTER THE THIRD EYE OPENING

Don't be surprised that when you awaken your third eye, you'll start getting unusual experiences. That especially has to do with your sight. When you're tired and you're about to sleep or you just relax and close your eyes, you may suddenly get all kinds of images in your mind's eye.

Some of them won't make any sense, some of them will be very vivid, others will be blurred... There are all kinds of dimensions out there and with your third eye opened you'll be able to pick up on them. The higher vibration you offer, the higher developed worlds you'll be able to explore.

If what you see is blurred it means your spiritual powers are still weak and you can't see non-physical things clearly.

HIGHER VS LOWER DIMENSIONS

If your vibration is low, you may get to see the dimensions where restless souls stay. By 'restless souls' I mean the souls of people who committed suicides and couldn't forgive themselves for having done that. They're afraid to be judged by someone, so they stay between this world and higher dimensions.

This, of course, is not the best dimension to choose to see, but if you find yourself viewing such dimension, you should understand that you offer the vibration that attracts such sights.

Although I have never seen lower dimensions, some people who saw them became scared and started regretting their third eye opening. Such people contact me asking what to do because they're scared of these sights.

All I can advise is to try to raise their vibration, because only then they'll be able to see higher dimensions. In general, you should become more positive to raise your vibration.

If you want to close your third eye, you can do so also. For this you need to ground yourself. You can do so by eating heavy food, playing team sports, talking to worldly people and avoiding spiritual practices for the time being. Warning: if you discontinue your spiritual practices it may take a very long time to get your spiritual powers back, if you developed any.

If you offer a very high vibration (that of peace, love, gratitude and happiness), you'll be able to see more developed worlds than the one in which we live. You'll know that you picked up on this kind of dimension if you see very vivid light colors and when the air seems to be full of golden light. Golden/white colors will be the main ones in these dimensions.

Sometimes it may seem to you that you get information overload, and you may not be able to tune out of these dimensions; they'll keep shifting through your eyes, sometimes really fast, different images may pass through you every second. Because you're new to this experience, you may not know how to switch off the third eye sight, so that might scare you.

Don't be afraid when that happens because all you should do is to open your eyes. You can also listen to the pleasant music before going to sleep and focus/touch something physical and that should turn off the third eye sight.

SENSITIVITY TO ENERGIES

After your third eye awakening you'll become more sensitive to the energies of other people. You'll be able to pick up on both good and bad energies. It's beneficial to pick up on good energies that others are offering, because they affect you positively.

However, you'll pick up on bad energies too. For example, if some person is angry and she looks at you, you're likely to get affected. That's why spiritual people sometimes get drained after spending some time in a crowded area. There are too many bad energies out there, and when you become more spiritual, you become more sensitive to such energies.

There are a few things you can do to reduce the harm of such energies. You can use some protection when you feel that you're among negative people. Such protection can be imagining that you're surrounded by white or golden (or both) light and imagining how their negative energy cannot get through that light. This is a very useful technique which I personally use. That always protects my personal gravity field.

You can also use another great technique that will benefit you in numerous ways. When you come home and take the shower, try to shower with cool water. Not too cold, but not as warm as you're used to. Now imagine that the water that goes on you is washing away all the bad energies that you picked up today. See in your mind's eye the water picking up such energies and taking them down with it.

When you do this exercise for a couple of days in a row, you'll feel a huge relief during and after the shower. The time you spend in the shower may become the most pleasurable one. Don't be surprised if after the shower you'll become extremely happy or inspired to do something. That's the result of removing negative energies from your body.

You should try doing this activity every day for you to feel the full benefits of this technique. When you do this every day you'll notice a huge difference in your daily energy levels. You'll be much more energetic and focused throughout the day because there will be no negative energies disrupting your routine.

Your health will improve significantly and your life quality will improve too. Your relationships, sleep, work and state of mind will improve to a great extent.

OTHER THIRD EYE OPENING EXPERIENCES

After your third eye opening you may get very strong vibrations in your body that may really scare you. It surely scared me when it happened to me the first time. I had no idea what's happening with me and I suspected that I'm about to have an OBE (out-of-body experience) because I read that something similar happens before such experience.

However, if you stay calm and just let the vibration overtake you, it will pass. During this vibration you may be able to see with your third eye or (if you still didn't awaken it) this experience may open your third eye.

I was able to get a glimpse only into higher dimensions, with beautiful houses and golden sunny days. The view that I get when I look through my third eye is a very interesting one. For example, I may see a detail of the house (e.g., two windows of the house and an edge of the roof and the sky). It's as though I am looking through a telescope. There's a pitch black color on the edges, and in the middle I see some sight.

Usually I see still objects, like houses and also people, creatures similar to people (nothing scary, trust me). I usually get a glimpse into the worlds that are very similar to that of ours. So people are similar and where they live is similar to where we live.

I'm not sure why I get only these experiences, I suspect that it's because I'm not ready to view very different worlds to that of ours.

As I mentioned earlier, you may also get a sight of a black sky with many stars. If you get such view it means that you got into the 4th dimension and that you may get into different worlds from this place. I cannot be any more clearer than this because I still didn't manage to clearly get into different worlds from this place. When I get smoother transition I'll definitely write a post about it.

HOW LONG IT TAKES TO EXPERIENCE THE THIRD EYE OPENING

The time it takes to open your third eye is different for everyone. If you were spiritually advanced in previous lives, or were trying to advance spiritually, it may take a very short while for you to experience your third eye opening. For me it took only around a week to do that, but I strongly feel that it's because I was spiritual in my previous life and I had many lives before this one.

You may need to wait from a week to two months for your third eye opening experience, sometimes even longer.

I hope that I didn't discourage you from the third eye opening. Although the experiences that you'll get after your third eye awakening are quite different from what you experience in this physical world, if you keep your vibration high you won't see anything of negative nature.

Therefore you should stay as positive as you can every day and if you do that you'll definitely enjoy the sights that you get because of your third eye.

If you're ready to open your third eye, read this:

THIRD EYE CHAKRA

Out of the main seven chakras third eye chakra is one of the most important ones. Your third eye gives you an opportunity to experience different dimensions without having to leave your body.

This is the easiest way to see other dimensions which your physical sight cannot perceive.

You see through your eyes the physical world and you also have the ability to see the spiritual world through your third eye chakra.

Third eye chakra has the purple/indigo color, however some people even see very dark, almost black eye. The eye doesn't even have to be shaped like an eye, although this is the most common shape. Some people see the third eye chakra shaped like a square or a star.

You can also see a realistic eye or just a shape filled with indigo or purple color.

If you don't get enough source energy it will be quite hard for your to open your third eye. You can get an abundance of universal energy by meditating. When you meditate you get universal energy through your crown chakra into your whole body.

Usually people experience their third eye when they meditate, and that certainly happened to me too. Through meditation you can get many experiences which include the awakening of kundalini energy, nervous system cleansing and the opening of the third eye chakra.

When you meditate your third eye may show itself to you without you even trying. However, if you consciously want to see it, you should, during meditation, concentrate on your third eye area (between your brows). However, you should not focus on this area too intensely. You just have to be aware of that area.

When you concentrate on your third eye area, you'll start feeling a tingling sensation or a slight pressure/vibration in that area. This always means that the third eye chakra is awakening, no matter how small pressure/vibration you're experiencing.

After some days, or even the same day of you trying to see the third eye, you may start seeing the colors of it. You may straight away become aware of your third eye, but that doesn't happen often.

Usually people start seeing blurry shapes and colors of gray, white, purple and indigo before the actual sight of the third eye chakra.

The more you meditate and practice, the stronger colors get and then you'll finally be able to see your third eye.

If you don't feel any vibration when you concentrate on the third eye, but you see colors of your third eye straight away, that means your third eye is already awakened.

This usually happens to people who were very spiritually advanced in their previous lives. Therefore in this life you don't need to try hard to develop spiritually -– everything happens very quickly and naturally.

When you see your third eye, you should concentrate on the middle of it or on the most intensely colored part of it. This way you'll get a glimpse of other worlds because you'll be sucked into the fourth dimension.

When that happens, you may feel being physically drawn to it, or you may feel vibration/pressure in your body. Don't get scared -— this is perfectly normal.

When you're getting sucked into the fourth dimension, you may experience your journey as going through a tunnel.

I personally saw a black tunnel and a beautiful purple light at the end of it. I was being sucked in very fast and I would constantly emerge from different tunnels.

When you concentrate on the light at the end of the tunnel, this pushes you forward and you can visit different worlds in different dimensions.

When you open your third eye chakra you become more spiritually sensitive because your aura gets a purple color. With time you'll be able to strengthen your personal gravity field so that you would be protected from the harmful energies of others.

With the opening of your third eye chakra your sixth sense sharpens and you become more in tune with the universe. Your personal traits may not change much, but you'll have a greater knowledge of this world and others.

Your eyesight lets you see the world through limiting beliefs, therefore you only see a small picture of the real world. Your third eye chakra doesn't have such filters, therefore you see the reality as it really is.

You'll benefit in many ways if you decide to awaken your third eye chakra. Your sixth sense will sharpen, therefore you'll become more sensitive to what's happening in your reality.

You'll also become more present in your daily activities which will empower you to complete them in a more effective way.

Furthermore, you'll understand that there's no such thing as death in this world -– after the end of your physical body your soul becomes connected to the whole of who you are.

When you open your third eye chakra, you'll be able to see other dimensions whilst being in your physical body. This will give you a better understanding of who you are and what your life's purpose is.

THIRD EYE – FAQ

Third Eye is a powerful tool of the Self to 'see', to 'hear' and to 'feel' altered frequency realities.

WHEN THIRD EYE GETS ACTIVATED?

Third Eye gets activated when one reaches Meditative State. One can reach Meditative State by transcending the body-mind consciousness. This happens in Meditation initially. As we practice more and more Meditation, Meditative state can be achieved even during normal waking state. So, Third Eye gets activated in Meditation and in Meditative state.

HOW TO ACTIVATE THIRD EYE?

Third Eye can not be activated by mind. So, one fails to activate Third Eye if he uses mind to activate Third Eye through certain techniques. Activation of Third Eye happens naturally in No Mind State or Meditative State. So, one has to practice more and more Meditation. As he gets more and more Energy in Meditation, his Third Eye gets activated. Third Eye activation has to happen only in Self state. So, one has to be with Self to achieve activation of Third Eye. Every one of us has Third Eye. We can perceive it in Self state. Every one can attain Third Eye activation.

IS THERE A TECHNIQUE TO ACTIVATE THIRD EYE?

The only way to activate Third Eye is to transcend the body-mind consciousness. For this there are various methods. These methods are called 'techniques'. One can chant 'Manthra' or one can meditate on a 'vision' or one can practice 'Pranayama'. In all these techniques, the common phenomenon is 'Observation'. Observation is the way to transcend mind. What ever technique one practices, he has to just 'Observe', just 'witness'. Slowly your doing stops, witnessing begins.

Then 'seeing' begins. Activation of Third Eye starts. The most profound technique is 'Observation of Breath'. Breath happens naturally with out mind. So, by observing the natural flow of Breath, one can easily transcends the body-mind consciousness.

He will be with the Self. Then his Third Eye gets activated.

HOW LONG WILL IT TAKES TO ACTIVATE ONE'S THIRD EYE?

Activation of Third Eye is beyond time and space. When you reach Meditative State and if you have intent to perceive Third Eye, then you will accumulate sufficient Cosmic Energy to activate Third Eye. At this stage one's Third Eye gets activated. To achieve Third Eye activation, Meditate intent fully for longer hours. One may experience Third Eye activation in one sitting also. It is your urge, intent and effort that makes sooner or later.

What are the experiences of Third Eye?

When our Third Eye gets activated, we will experience one or more of the following Third Eye experiences. We 'feel' an itching sensation at our forehead region. We 'feel' pulling sensation at our forehead region. We 'feel' swirling sensation at our forehead region. We 'see' colors- colors like blue, green, pink, yellow and many more combination of vibrant colors. We 'see' rotation of colors in different directions. One 'see' colors as clouds moving.We 'see' big blank black screen.We 'see' pitch dark in a moving form, moving like a tunnel.We 'hear' sounds, sounds of walking.We 'hear' sounds of music instruments.We 'hear' voices of Masters as messages.We 'feel' the presence of Master.We 'see' crystal clear images of places, animals, persons-known or unknown.We 'see' other frequency realities.We 'see' bright light. Light may 'fee' like Master.We 'see', 'hear' and 'feel' so many things which we can not express with words.

WHAT UNDERSTANDING ONE GETS THROUGH THIRD EYE EXPERIENCES?

Third Eye Experiences are one of the great experiences for a Meditator.Through Third Eye experiences, we understand the Beyond.We will get answers for our problems through messages of Masters or as 'feel'.We start understanding that we are not just body and mind with senses.We start perceiving Extra Sensory Perception. With these experiences, Our actions will change.Our perception will change.Our understandings will change.We start understanding the Unlimitedness.

THIRD EYE CHAKRA HEALING

WHAT IS THIRD EYE CHAKRA HEALING

The Third Eye Chakra – also called the Sixth Chakra, and Brow Chakra, and Ajna Chakra – is located between the eyebrows in the center of the brain. The pituitary gland, hypothalamus, and the autonomic nervous system, are governed by the third eye chakra. It is the energy center for our "sixth sense", intuitive perception, psychic abilities, and visualization. The third eye chakra is associated the element Light, the sense of Intuition, and the color Indigo.

Third eye chakra healing is about having control of how to open and close the third eye. Brow chakra healing will open up your psychic abilities – clairvoyance (seeing), clairaudience (hearing), clairsentience (feeling), and claircognizance (knowing/clear thought). Third eye opening is about being able to receive intuitive information, and about having a greater control over your mind and emotions. When your third eye chakra is awakened and balanced you will experience high mental ability, clear thinking, focus, and good health. You will also be able to combine emotion and logic, and separate imagination from reality. Having your third eye opening can also help with fatigue, sleep problems, day dreaming, disorientation, inability to listen to others, empathy of others, and gaining self confidence.

HOW TO OPEN AND HEAL THE THIRD EYE CHAKRA

When your sixth chakra Ajna, has been blocked for a longer period, you will begin to experience emotional and/or physical health problems (see symptoms of a blocked brow chakra below). Third eye chakra healing will open, awaken, and balance your sixth chakra Ajna. You will begin to allow the life force to flow freely again with third eye opening healing sessions.

Opening the third eye chakra will not only cure the symptoms, it will also heal the root problems! As your sixth chakra is balanced, it will positively affect the other chakras as well since they work as one system. This means that the healing benefits from third eye opening will appear in several areas of your life.

There are different third eye opening techniques, and we have gathered some of the most effective and powerful healing techniques that you can apply on yourself to awaken and balance your sixth chakra Ajna:

* Affirmations

* Third Eye Chakra Stones & Crystals

* Essential Oils

* Foods

* Ajna Yoga

* Third Eye Meditation – Ajna Chakra Meditation

* Sound Healing

So, what problems can these third eye opening techniques assist you with? What are the sings of a blocked brow chakra?

HOW CAN THIRD EYE CHAKRA HEALING BE OF HELP? THIRD EYE OPENING BENEFITS?

Third chakra healing can help you with headaches, migraines, sleeping problems, fatigue, dizziness, day dreaming, and disorientation. Opening your third eye can also assist in increasing your self confidence. Your listening skills will improve and you will become more empathetic with third eye opening sessions. Improved memory, improved learning ability, and enhanced intuition, are also benefits of awakening the third eye. When you are in the process of opening the third eye chakra you will start experiencing higher states of consciousness and receive guidance from your higher self and Spirits.

Signs of an imbalanced brow chakra or Ajna chakra include: headaches, migraines, dizziness, nausea, learning disabilities, panic, depression, seizures, tumors, brain cysts, problems with eyesight, hearing, balance, and the spinal cord. Make sure to seek medical attention if you are having any of these symptoms. Third eye chakra healing is not a medical treatment, but a complimentary healing method.

DO YOU NEED THIRD EYE CHAKRA HEALING / THIRD EYE OPENING?

You could really benefit from applying some of the third eye opening techniques described below, if you suffer from low self confidence, headaches, migraines, nausea, dizziness, panic attacks, hearing problems, eyesight problems, or depression. Also, if you have learning difficulties, lack common sense, need to improve your listening skills, lack empathy, are judgmental, are over intellectual, or don't listen to your intuition, you probably need third eye chakra healing, as these problems are related to the sixth chakra Ajna.

DO YOU HAVE A BALANCED, DEFICIENT, OR AN EXCESSIVE THIRD EYE CHAKRA?

If you experience any of the third eye chakra imbalance symptoms mentioned above, you either have a deficient energy, or an excessive energy in your sixth chakra Ajna. Learn about the general characteristics of a balanced, deficient, and excessive third eye chakra and find out which you have:

A balanced third eye chakra: learn things easily, have great memory, determined, strong will power, intuitive, receive messages from spirit guides, open to a higher consciousness & wisdom, connected to your Divinity and fully understand how to be/do/have anything you want, have out of body experiences / astral travel

A deficient third eye chakra: difficulty in learning things, inability to focus, bad memory, no connection between outer reality and your inner world, no spiritual understanding, no common sense, lacking intuition, have little or no empathy to others An excessive third eye chakra: stressed, suffer from headaches /migraines, judgmental, over-intellectual, overpowering others, unsympathetic, living in a fantasy world, delusional, hallucinating.

If you have a deficient or excessive third eye chakra, it can be a good idea to heal the sixth chakra as the healing process will balance the energy in this center. The following third eye chakra healing techniques & tools will open, awaken, balance and heal the sixth chakra Ajna: affirmations, third eye chakra stones & crystals, essential oils, foods, Ajna yoga, third eye meditation / Ajna chakra meditation, and sound healing.

Learn about the different third eye chakra opening and awakening techniques and choose the ones that you feel guided to. Remember that the healing process should never be "work". Make the healing process of the sixth chakra fresh and fun. Alternate between the different techniques, and enjoy the healing benefits!

THIRD EYE OPENING & HEALING – AFFIRMATIONS

Third eye chakra healing affirmations can be helpful in opening, awakening, and balancing the sixth chakra Ajna. You will connect to a higher consciousness as you state these powerful affirmations on a regular basis described below. Work with the ones that resonate with your sixth chakra (brow chakra). Write down the third eye opening & healing affirmations, and place them where you can see them often – on the fridge, on the mirror, on your computer, in your wallet, in your car, in your office, in your locker etc. Make sure to only do your third eye chakra healing affirmations when you feel good, since you affirm with your vibration.

I am wise, intuitive and connected with my inner guide

I am in touch with my inner guidance

I listen to the wisdom within me

I trust my intuition to guide and protect me

I understand the "big picture"

I always understand the true meaning of life situations

I know that all is well in my world

I trust that whatever comes to me is for my greatest joy and highest good

I am open to inspiration and bliss

I imagine, I envision, I dream, I know, I see

I am perfectly attuned to my vision

I move toward my vision with purpose and clarity

I am connected to my Divinity

I am at peace

THIRD EYE CHAKRA STONES & CRYSTALS

Crystal healing is often applied by energy healers for third eye opening and balancing. The color of the third eye chakra (brow chakra) is indigo; the color of spirituality and wisdom. This is why many third eye chakra stones and crystals have the color indigo/purple.

You can also use third eye chakra stones on yourself, to open and balance your sixth chakra Ajna. Wear these lovely third eye crystals as jewelry, or place them under your pillow as you sleep, and enjoy the healing benefits at the same time! However, another way that is probably more effective for third eye opening is to use them during meditation. Next time you meditate, place the healing stone on your sixth chakra. Visualize how the color indigo is vibrating on your third eye chakra (brow chakra), and imagine how your third eye chakra opens up. Below are examples of powerful third eye chakra stones and crystals that you can use to open and balance your sixth chakra Ajna:

amethyst	labrodite
azurite	lapiz lazuli
blue aventurine	lolite
blue fluorite	opal
blue sapphire	purple fluorite
blue tourmaline	sodalite
kyanite	tanzanite

THIRD EYE OPENING & HEALING – ESSENTIAL OILS

Working with essential oils for third eye opening and third eye chakra healing is a lovely way to relax and enjoy the healing benefits at the same time. Your memory, learning ability, intelligence, common sense, and intuition will improve, as your sixth chakra Ajna (third eye chakra / brow chakra) becomes more balanced.

Awakening the third eye chakra doesn't need to be difficult. Just add a few drops into your bath, mix a few drops with your massage oil, or use an oil burner / diffuser. Below are examples of essential oils that can be very powerful for third eye opening and third eye chakra healing:

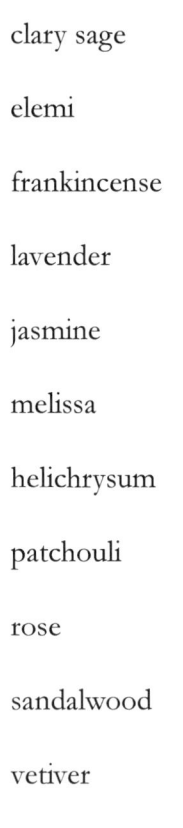

- clary sage
- elemi
- frankincense
- lavender
- jasmine
- melissa
- helichrysum
- patchouli
- rose
- sandalwood
- vetiver

THIRD EYE OPENING & HEALING – FOODS

There are certain foods that can fuel the third eye chakra (brow chakra). Third eye chakra healing foods are often purple or dark blue in color, and they nourish the brain and mood. Here are examples on what you can eat and drink to awaken your sixth chakra / third eye chakra.

acai berries

blackberries

blueberries

chocolate

cranberries

eggplants

grape juice

lavender spice

mugwort

pomegranate

poppy seed

raspberries

red grapes

red wine

THIRD EYE OPENING & HEALING – AJNA YOGA

Yoga is very effective for third eye opening and awakening. The sixth chakra or Ajna Chakra, is both the perception and command center. It is from here you recall past events or last night's dream, and it is also from here you imagine, visualize, and create and your future. There are certain Ajna Yoga poses that can help optimizing your brain functions. These Ajna positions will also open your sixth chakra and allow the life force to flow to the other chakras as well. This means that your overall health will start to improve. As the third eye chakra (brow chakra) is awakened and balanced, your intuition and psychic abilities will develop. You will open up to a higher consciousness and wisdom, and connect to your own Divinity.

The following Ajna Yoga poses are very powerful for third eye opening and awakening. They will balance your sixth chakra Ajna:

THE CHILD POSE – BALASANA

The Child pose, or Balasana, is great for third eye awakening as it stimulates the sixth chakra Ajna. Furthermore, this Ajna Yoga pose calms the brain, and relieves stress, fatigue, back pain and neck pain. It also stretches the hips, thighs and ankles.

STANDING HALF FORWARD BEND – ARDHA UTTANASANA

Standing Half Forward Bend, or Ardha Uttanasana, is a great Ajna Yoga pose as it stimulates and puts pressure on the third eye chakra (brow chakra). Besides awakening the sixth chakra, it will also improve posture and strengthen the back. Furthermore, this Ajna Yoga pose will stretch the front torso and stimulate the belly.

THE SHOULDER STAND POSE – SARVANGASANA

The Shoulder Stand, or Sarvangasana, is a fantastic Ajna Yoga pose as it opens the sixth chakra (third eye chakra) and allows the blood to flow directly into the neck and head. This Ajna Yoga pose comes with many health benefits. It stretches the shoulders and neck, tones the buttocks and legs, improves digestion, helps with fatigue and insomnia, stimulates the thyroid and prostate glands, helps relieve the symptoms of menopause. Furthermore, this Ajna Yoga pose can help with infertility, asthma, sinusitis, and mild depression.

THIRD EYE MEDITATION – AJNA CHAKRA MEDITATION

Third eye meditation, or Ajna chakra meditation is very powerful for third eye opening and balancing. You will connect to a higher wisdom and guidance as your sixth chakra Ajna is balanced. As you apply Ajna chakra meditation, try and visualize the color indigo; the color of the third eye chakra (brow chakra). Imagine how an indigo light is vibrating in your sixth chakra Ajna, and how it opens the third eye chakra.

Below are third eye meditation / Ajna chakra meditation videos that you can use to awaken, clear and balance your sixth chakra (brow chakra):

THIRD EYE OPENING & HEALING – SOUND HEALING

Sound healing can be very powerful for third eye opening and balancing. As your sixth chakra Ajna is awakened you will connect to your higher consciousness and your psychic powers. The third eye chakra (brow chakra) resonates with a specific color, note, and Hz:

Color Indigo – Note A – 852 Hz

Solfeggio frequencies is a sound healing tool that can be very effective in awakening the third eye chakra. The solfeggio frequency for the third eye chakra (brow chakra) is at 741 Hz. This frequency is about connecting to your spirituality and opening up to a higher consciousness and guidance. Listen to this third eye chakra healing frequency (see videos below) on a regular basis to open and balance your sixth chakra Ajna. It's best to use headphones for optimal healing benefits. Enjoy!

BENEFITS OF OPENING YOUR THIRD EYE

Here are a lot of benefits from the decalcification or activation of your third eye or also called your pineal gland. I see a lot of people are wondering how to know their third eye is opened or decalcified.

Our everyday life leads to calcification of the third eye and therefore, it doesn't work at its full potential by producing DMT and connecting us to other worlds.

If you have successfully decalcified and activated your third eye, you should observe a lot of benefits.

I have listed some of the most popular benefits of third eye activation.

BENEFITS OF OPENING YOUR THIRD EYE.

A lot of people believe that the third eye functions as a spiritual gateway through which you can see beyond time and space. In short, activating the third eye, your perceptions exceed the limits of the material, physical word and the mind awakens and connects you to levels of being where time doesn't exist. And this leads to a number of great advantages:

1. GREATER AWARENESS / AWAKENING.

Advantages of awakening your third eye. Awakening your third eye metaphysically opens our eyes from a deep spiritual lethargy. This allows us to begin to perceive the "truth" that surrounds us.

What this means is that you will begin to see the world we live in is full of control and inequality and is not in harmony with the rest of the Universe.

You will feel a desire to be free and live in a world filled with love, compassion and truth. Eventually, you will feel and see the interconnectedness with everything around you in nature and will feel a deep connection with the Universe.

This is a deep sense that allows you to see the beauty in all things and to realize that your physical I is not your true nature.

2. PSYCHIC POWERS / EMPATHY.

Your instincts are as a well-adjusted compass that points you in the "right" direction to achieve what your soul is looking for.

With activating the pineal gland, you are able to read instinctive signals far easier until they become almost like another sense, hence the term sixth sense is derived from.

It's almost like you know what will happen and what will be the results of certain events. That's why some people think that the most notable prophets of our time had their third eye opened.

The feeling that we are all part of the same whole also becomes clear and you are capable of empathy with others, knowing that they are part of the same universal consciousness.

3. LAWS OF ATTRACTION / SPACE ORDER.

Opening your third eye chakra. As a result of the opened third eye, the third eye chakra is activated, which in turn will help to balance your chakra system.

When you are energized and in harmony with the Universe, you are like a giant magnet for events, people, situations etc. By harnessing the power of the positive intent, gratitude and love, you can manifest much more beauty in your life. You will notice that the number of useful "coincidences" will be greatly increased.

4. VIVID DREAMS / LUCID DREAMING.

Since your pineal gland regulates your sleep cycles, you will find that you sleep much better and that your dreams are more vivid and you're lucid dreaming. This means that you will feel that you can control your dreams and you will be able to realize your true infinite self and the infinite possibilities that exist in a state of sleep.

Additionally, you will realize that this world of dreams is the same as the "real world" in which we live, for example the fact that we have unlimited possibilities and we are all masters of our own universe.

5. ASTRAL TRAVEL / ASTRAL PROJECTION.

When the third eye connects to this level of existence where there is no time and space, our soul is able to rise above the physical body and astral travel in time and space.

Astral projection is one of the benefits coming with the activation of your third eye. It has the ability to go anywhere in the universe and at any time in the universe.

Many people belive that when we dream, we actually astral travel, and with fully opened third eye we are able to astral travel while we are awake, for example, when we meditate.

6. IMAGINATION / CREATIVITY.

With activated pineal gland, you are continuously connected to the plane of existence where our souls reside.

In the plane of existence, there is no time or space, just an endless love and truth – everything that has happened and will ever happen already exists in the plane of existence.

After connecting to it, you will find that your imagination and creativity are super charged and you are able to find solutions to problems easier because all the solutions to all problems already exist in this place. Along with the ability to have vivid dreams and lucid dreaming, this will spark your imagination to a whole new level.

Made in the USA
Monee, IL
02 February 2021